9-1 GCSE NOTES FOR WILLIAM GOLDING'S *LORD OF THE FLIES* - Study guide (All chapters, page-by-page analysis)

by Joe Broadfoot

The right of Joe Broadfoot to be identified as the author of this work has been asserted in accordance with Section 77 of the Copyright, Designs and Patents Act 1988

ISBN-13:
978-1537459363

ISBN-10:
1537459368

9-1 GCSE REVISION NOTES – LORD OF THE FLIES

CONTENTS

Introduction 3
Best essay practice 4
Essay planning 5
New specification 8
Chapter One 14
Chapter Two 21
Chapter Three 25
Chapter Four 28
Chapter Five 32
Chapter Six 37
Chapter Seven 41
Chapter Eight 44
Chapter Nine 49
Chapter Ten 52
Chapter Eleven 55
Chapter Twelve 58
Essay Writing Tips 62
Glossary 67

Brief Introduction

This book is aimed at GCSE students of English Literature who are studying William Golding's *Lord of the Flies*. The focus is on what examiners are looking for, especially since the changes to the curriculum in 2015, and here you will find each chapter covered in detail. I hope this will help you and be a valuable tool in your studies and revision.

Criteria for high marks

Make sure you use appropriate critical language (see glossary of literary terms at the back). You need your argument to be fluent, well-structured and coherent. Stay focused!

Analyse and explore the use of form, structure and the language. Explore how these aspects affect the meaning.

Make connections between texts and look at different interpretations. Explore their strengths and weaknesses. Don't forget to use supporting references to strengthen your argument.

Analyse and explore the context.

Best essay practice

There are so many way to write an essay. Many schools use **PEE** for paragraphs: point/evidence/explain. Others use **PETER**: point/evidence/technique/explain/reader; **PEEL**: point, example, explain, link; **PEEE**: point/evidence/explain/explore. Whichever method you use, make sure you mention the **writer's effects**. This generally is what most students forget to add. You must think of what the writer is trying to achieve by using a particular technique and what is actually achieved. Do not just spot techniques and note them. You may get some credit for using appropriate technology, but unless you can comment on the effect created on the reader and/or the writer's intention, you will miss out on most of the marks available.

Essay planning

In order to write a good essay it is necessary to plan. In fact, it is best to quite formulaic in an exam situation, as you won't have much time to get started. Therefore I will ask you to learn the following acronym: **DATMC (Definition, Application, Terminology, Main, Conclusion**. Some schools call it: **GSLMC (General, Specific, Link, Main, Conclusion)**, but it amounts to the same thing. The first three letters concern the introduction. (Of course, the alternative is to leave some blank lines and write your introduction after you have completed the main body of your essay, but it is probably not advisable for most students).

Let us first look at the following exam question, which is on poetry (of course, the same essay-planning principles apply to essays on novels and plays as well).

QUESTION: Explore how the poet conveys **feelings** in the poem.

STEP ONE: Identify the **keyword** in the question. (I have already done this, by highlighting it in **bold**). If you are following GSLMC, you now need to make a **general statement** about what feelings are. Alternatively, if you're following DATMC, simply **define** 'feelings'. For example, 'Feelings are emotion states or reactions or vague, irrationals ideas and beliefs'.

STEP TWO: If you are following GSLMC, you now need to make a **specific statement** linking feelings (or whatever else you've defined) to how they appear in the poem. Alternatively, if you're following DATMC, simply define which 'feelings' **apply** in this poem. For example, 'The feelings love, fear and guilt appear in this poem, and are expressed by the speaker in varying degrees.'

STEP THREE: If you are following GSLMC, you now need to make a **link statement** identifying the methods used to convey the feelings (or whatever else you've defined) in the poem. Alternatively, if you're following DATMC, simply define which **techniques** are used to convey 'feelings' in this poem. For example, 'The poet primarily uses alliteration to emphasise his heightened emotional state, while hyperbole and enjambment also help to convey the sense that the speaker is descending into a state of madness.

STEP FOUR: Whether you are following GSLMC or DATMC, the next stage is more or less the same. The main part of the essay involves writing around **six paragraphs**, using whichever variation of PEEE you prefer. In my example, I will use **Point, Evidence, Exploration, Effect** on the listener. To make your essay even stronger, try to use your quotations chronologically. It will be easier for the examiner to follow, which means you are more likely to achieve a higher grade. To be more specific, I recommend that you take and analyse two quotations from the beginning of the poem, two from the middle, and two at the end.

STEP FIVE: Using Carol Ann Duffy's poem, 'Stealing', here's an example of how you could word one of your six paragraphs: **(POINT)** 'Near the beginning of the poem, the speaker's determination is expressed.' **(EVIDENCE)** 'This is achieved through the words: 'Better off dead than giving in'. **(EXPLORATION).** The use of 'dead' emphasizes how far the speaker is prepared to go in pursuit of what he wants, although there is a sense that he is exaggerating (hyperbole). **(EFFECT)** The listener senses that the speaker may be immature given how prone he is to exaggerate his own bravery.

STEP SIX: After writing five or more paragraphs like the one above, it will be time to write a **conclusion**. In order to do that, it is necessary to sum up your previous points and evaluate them. This is not the time to introduce additional quotations. Here is an example of what I mean: 'To conclude, the poet clearly conveys the speaker's anger. Although the listener will be reluctant to completely sympathise with a thief, there is a sense that the speaker is suffering mentally, which makes him an interesting and partially a sympathetic character. By using a dramatic monologue form, the poet effectively conveys the speaker's mental anguish, which makes it easier to more deeply understand what first appears to be inexplicable acts of violence.

Other tips

Make your studies active!

Don't just sit there reading! Never forget to annotate, annotate and annotate!

All page references refer to the 1958 paperback edition of *Lord of the Flies* published by Faber and Faber, London (ISBN: 978-0-571-19147-5).

Lord of the Flies

AQA (New specification starting in 2015)

If you're studying for an AQA qualification in English Literature, there's a good chance your teachers will choose this text to study. There are good reasons for that: it's moralistic in that the text encourages us to think about right and wrong.

Lord of the Flies is one of the texts listed on Paper 2. This paper needs to be completed in 2 hours 15 minutes. Your writing on the essay will only be part of the exam, however, and for the rest of time you will need to write about poetry: two poems categorised as 'Unseen Poetry' and two poems from the AQA anthology.

AQA have given students a choice of 12 set texts for the Modern Texts section of the exam paper. There are 6 plays: JB Priestley's *An Inspector Calls*, Willy Russell's

Blood Brothers, Alan Bennett's *The History Boys*, Dennis Kelly's *DNA*, Simon Stephens's script of *The Curious Incident of the Dog* in the *Night-Time*, and Shelagh Delaney's *A Taste of Honey*. Alternatively, students can chose to write on the following 6 novels: William Golding's *Lord of the Flies*, AQA's Anthology called *Telling Tales*, George Orwell's *Animal Farm*, Kazuo Ishiguro's *Never Let Me Go*, Meera Syal's *Anita and Me*, and Stephen Kelman's *Pigeon English*. Answering one essay question on one of the above is worth a total of 34 marks, which includes 4 for vocabulary, spelling, punctuation and grammar. In other words, this section is worth 21.25% of your total grade at GCSE.

AQA have produced a poetry anthology entitled *Poems, Past and Present*, which includes 30 poems. Rather than study all 30, students are to study one of the two clusters of 15, which concentrate on common themes. There are two themes which students can choose from: Love and relationships, or power and conflict. Within the chosen thematic cluster, students must study all 15 poems and be prepared to write on any of them. Answering this section is worth 18.75% of your total GCSE grade.

The 'unseen poetry' section is more demanding, in that students will not know what to expect. However, as long as they are prepared to comment and compare different poems in terms of their content, theme, structure and language, students should be ready for whatever the exam can throw at them. This section is worth 20% of your total grade at GCSE.

Paper 2 itself makes up 60% of your total grade or, in other words, 96 raw marks. Just under half of those marks, 44 to be exact (27.5% of 60%), can be gained from analysing how the writer uses language, form and structure to create effects. To get a high grade, it is necessary for students to use appropriate literary terms, like metaphors, similes and so on.

AO1 accounts for 36 marks of the total of 96 (22.5% of the 60% for Paper 2, to be exact). To score highly on AO1, students need to provide an informed personal response, using quotations to support their point of view.

AO3 is all about context and, like Paper 1, only 7.5% of the total mark is awarded for this knowledge (12 marks). Similarly, AO4 (which is about spelling, punctuation and grammar) only accounts for 2.5% of the total (4 marks).

Let's consider Paper One now, as it's also important. One of the difficulties with Paper 1 is the language. That can't be helped, bearing in mind that part A of the exam paper involves answering questions on Shakespeare, whereas part B is all about the 19th-century novel.

To further complicate things, the education system is in a state of flux: that means we have to be ready for constant change. Of course, everyone had got used to grades A,B and C meaning a pass. It was simple, it was straightforward and nearly everyone understood it. Please be prepared that from this day henceforward, the top grade will now be known as 9. A grade 4 will be a pass, and anything below that will be found and anything above it will be a pass. Hopefully, that's not too confusing for anyone!

Now onto the exam itself. As I said, Paper 1 consists of Shakespeare and the 19th-century novel. Like Paper 2, it is a written closed-book exam (in other words you are not allowed to have the texts with you), which lasts one hour 45 minutes. You can score 64 marks, which amounts to 40% of your GCSE grade.

In section B, students will be expected to write in detail about an extract from the novel they have studied in class and then write about the novel as a whole. Just for the record, the choices of novel are the following: *The Strange Case of Dr Jekyll and Mr Hyde* by Robert Louis Stevenson, *A Christmas Carol* and *Great Expectations* by Charles Dickens, *Jane Eyre* by Charlotte Brontë, *Frankenstein* by Mary Shelley, *Pride and Prejudice* by Jane Austin, and *The Sign of Four* by Sir Arthur Conan Doyle.

Another important thing to consider is the fact that for section B of Paper 1, you will not be assessed on Assessment Objective 4 (AO4), which involves spelling, punctuation, grammar and vocabulary. This will be assessed on section A of Paper 1, which is about Shakespeare, and it will be worth 2.5% of your overall GCSE grade. In terms of raw marks, it is worth 4 out of 64. So for once, we need not concern ourselves with what is affectionately known as 'SPAG' too much on this part of Paper 1.

However, it is necessary to use the correct literary terminology wherever possible to make sure we maximise our marks on Assessment Objective2 (AO2). AO2 tests how well we can analyse language form and structure. Additionally, we are expected to state the effect the writer tried to create and how it impacts on the reader.

This brings me onto Assessment Objective 1 (AO1), which involves you writing a personal response to the text. It is important that you use quotations to backup your points of view. Like AO2, AO1 is worth 15% of your GCSE on Paper 1.

Assessment Objective 3 (AO3) is worth half of that, but nevertheless it is important to comment on context to make sure you get as much of the 7.5% up for grabs as you can.

So just to make myself clear, there are 30 marks available in section B for your answer on the 19th-century novel. Breaking it down even further, you will get 12 marks maximum the backing up your personal opinion with quotations, an additional 12 marks for analysing the writer's choice of words for effect (not forgetting to use appropriate terminology - more on that see the glossary at the back of this book), and six marks for discussing context.

As you can see, we've got a lot to get through so without further ado let's get on with the actual text itself and possible exam questions.

Previous exam questions

Notwithstanding the governmental changes to the grading system, it is still good practice to go over previous exam papers. To make sure that you meet AQA's learning objectives and get a high mark, make sure you go into the exam knowing something about the following:

- the plot

- the characters

- the theme

- selected quotations/details

- exam skills

Page-by-page analysis

Chapter One

The opening chapter is entitled: 'The Sound of the Shell' and the first character we encounter is unnamed (1). Not naming characters at the beginning makes the story work better on an allegorical level, as readers can absorb the universal message without the distraction of specific names.

'The boy with fair hair' is the first character we discover (1). He seems to be the victim of a hostile environment as we are told that 'the scar', which is a geological term referring to exposed rock but sounds like a physical wound on the skin, 'smashed into the jungle' (1). As well as being a violent pun, the scar is personified as attacking the jungle. It shows how threatening this place is.

Through sound imagery, we hear a human voice call out just after 'a witch-like cry' of a bird (1). It seems that humans will play second fiddle to animals in this hostile world and the second character is already portrayed as a victim, 'scratched by thorns' (1).

The second character has 'plump' knees and is 'shorter than the fair boy' (1). Additionally, we discover that he wears 'thick spectacles' (2). He is more talkative than the fair boy and uses UK slang, when he says: 'All them other kids', for instance (2).

The fair boy seems pleased that there are 'no grown-ups' (2). However, the plump boy is more anxious, thinking about the other boys that were on the plane that brought them to this place. By contrast, the fair boy is an optimist; he has no doubt that his father will 'be back' to pick them up (2).

The plump boy asks the fair boy his name and we discover it's Ralph. We have to wait longer to find out the name of the 'fat boy', but we do so over his a follower rather than a leader, as he 'hung steadily at' Ralph's 'shoulder' (3).

The fat boy is less reckless than Ralph, who trips 'over a branch' (3). Consequently, the fat boy tells Ralph that his 'auntie told' him 'not to run' because of his 'asthma' (3). We get the impression that the fat boy is physically weak in comparison to Ralph.

Yet the fat boy is more practical; he goes looking for 'fruit' (4). Meanwhile, the twelve-year-old Ralph enjoys the moment, laughing 'delightedly' (5). We discover that Ralph 'might make a boxer [...] but there was a mildness about his mouth and eyes that proclaimed no devil' (5). We get the impression of a physically strong and decent person.

However, Ralph is childish, as exemplified by his reaction to finding out that the fat boy's nickname was 'Piggy' (6). He mercilessly teases Piggy, who accepts it in good grace providing he doesn't 'tell the others' (6).

Piggy's cautious nature is revealed when 'carefully' disrobes before testing 'the water with one toe' (7). This contrasts vividly with Ralph's approach, which is just to dive in.

Ralph is enjoying the freedom of being away from parental control, while Piggy continually mentions his auntie. Ralph says: 'Sucks to your auntie!' (8). This shows how Ralph has little regard for Piggy and any wisdom he may be able to impart.

We discover that Ralph's father is 'a commander in the Navy' (8). Meanwhile, Piggy's 'dad's dead' and he struggles to mention what's happened to his mum (8). The virtually orphaned Piggy's been brought up by his 'auntie' (8). Charles Dickens often used orphans as main characters in his novels to increase the reader's sympathy for the protagonist.

Meanwhile, the environment is so hostile that even 'the lagoon attacked them with a blinding effulgence' (9). This shows how dazzled the two children are by their surroundings. A struggle for survival is expected as they have to endure 'the sun's enmity' (9).

Nevertheless, Ralph is a dreamy optimist and he ignores 'Piggy's ill-omened talk' (10). He spots 'a conch' in the lagoon and retrieves it (11). Piggy tells Ralph how 'expensive' the conch is and suggests using it to 'call the others' to 'have a meeting' (11, 12).

Once Ralph produces 'a strident blare' with the conch, other children begin to appear (13). We meet Johnny, who's described as 'sturdy and fair' with 'his face covered with a sticky mess of fruit' (13).

As more children appear, Piggy shows his responsible nature by moving 'among the crowd, asking names and frowning to remember them' (14). He is clearly taking his assumed responsibility seriously.

Something 'dark' appears in the distance, and eventually we see that 'the creature' is 'a party of boys' (15). There is something foreboding and almost Nazi-like about the approach of a group 'marching approximately in step' (15). We discover that 'the boy who controlled them was dressed in the same way though his cap was golden' (15). Uniform is clearly important and keeps this group in line.

The leader of the group is described as 'tall, thin, and bony' (16). He is also 'ugly', 'freckled' with blue eyes that are 'ready to turn, to anger' (16). Already, the reader may feel that this character may threaten the relatively peaceful nature of the scene so far.

We discover that the leader's surname is 'Merridew' (16). This name sounds 'merry', but actually he is merciless with a 'fallen boy', who he says is 'always throwing a faint' (16).

Merridew reveals that his first name is 'Jack' (17). His harsh nature is further revealed when he says to Piggy: 'Shut up, Fatty' (17). This comment and the 'storm of laughter' that arises after the children discover Piggy's nickname establishes the fat boy as an outsider. This is further emphasised by the 'closed circuit of sympathy with Piggy outside' that is established (17-18).

'The dark boy, Roger' sensibly suggests that they should have a 'vote for chief' (18). Ralph wins on account of his 'stillness', 'his size, and attractive appearance' (19). Additionally, there is his possession of the conch, which appears to be nine tenths of the law here. However, Ralph is magnanimous in victory, telling Jack: 'The choir belongs to you, of course' (19).

Jack and Ralph develop a 'shy liking' for each other and, with Simon, they decide to 'go on an expedition' to find out more about where they are (20). Simon is the boy who fainted earlier and is described as 'a skinny,vivid little boy, with a glance coming up from under a hut of straight hair that hung down, black and coarse' (20).

Piggy wants to come to, but Ralph tells him that he is 'no good on a job like this' (21). However, we discover Piggy is determined for he hangs on 'bumbling behind them'

(21). Ralph eventually looks at Piggy with 'more understanding', which implies he is slowly learning leadership qualities (21). He instructs Piggy to 'go back [...] and take names' (22).

The three explorers negotiate the 'pink cliffs' and notice 'narrow tracks' (23). Jack insists these tracks must have been made by 'animals' (23). The boys are likened to 'pliant needles' as they make their way through the undergrowth (23). The word 'pliant' suggests that while they are being flexible, it could mean they they are easily influenced; 'needles' implies that they have to become sharp and possibly spiteful to survive.

Ralph's immaturity rises to the surface again, as he pretends 'to knock Simon down' (24). However, he regains his sense of responsibility, as he commands the other two with the words: 'Got to get on' (24).

The boys decide to push a rock down the cliff. It is described as 'large as a small motor car' (25). This reminds the reader of how the boys are more at home in a motorised urban environment than a jungle. When the rock falls it shakes the the forest 'as with the passage of an enraged monster' (25). Again, this reminds the reader of how dangerous their surrounding are, as even a rock can create devastation.

Nevertheless, the boys take ownership of the island, as Ralph declares: 'This belongs to us' (26). Their insignificance in the greater scheme of things is made obvious by the 'insect-like figures' they see on the platform 'jutting into the lagoon'; these are the other boys, observed from above (27).

The boys have the opportunity to kill 'a piglet caught in a curtain of creepers' (28). The alliteration of the letter 'c' draws attention to the sentence, which shows how significant this moment is. Jack has a knife with him, but although he raises it to strike, he can't. Jack explains he 'was choosing a place' to strike (29). Just to show there will be 'no mercy' next time, Jack 'snatched his knife out of the sheath and slammed it into a tree trunk' (29). This act foreshadows the violence which will come later in the novel.

Chapter Two

In the chapter entitled: 'Fire on the Mountain', we discover that Ralph is not as confident as he first appears (30) When addressing the rest of the boys at the afternoon meeting, he feels 'uncertain whether to stand up or remain sitting' (30). He looks to Piggy for reassurance, but his fat ally offers 'no help' (30).

Ralph's speech with the conch is interrupted by Jack, who insists that 'you need an army - for hunting' (31). Jack's call for action may sound more appealing than Ralph's negative summing up of the situation that they find themselves in: 'No houses, no smoke, no footprints, no boats, no people' (30). What's more Jack backs up his words with gestures, as when he slams 'his knife into a trunk' (31).

Rather than let matters escalate out of control, Ralph suggests having '"Hands up" like at school' (31). However, the difference is he will 'give the conch to the next person to speak' (31). He adds that the speaker 'won't be interrupted' unless it's by Ralph, himself (31).

Jack is keen on 'rules', as he seems to be looking forward to disciplining 'anyone' who 'breaks 'em' (32). Ralph manages to subtly calm Jack down, who seems to be considering interrupting Piggy, who now has the conch

(32). Once again, Ralph displays a growing maturity by patting 'the log' to get Jack to sit down (32).

The 'breathless' Piggy pessimistically predicts that they 'may be' on the island 'a long time' (32). Ralph looks on the bright side, saying: 'While we are waiting we can have a good time on this island' (33). The boys are quick to imagine it to be 'like in a book' as, judging by their outbursts, they've been avid readers of 'Treasure Island', 'Swallows and Amazons' and 'Coral Island' (33). In short, they have a romantic view of their situation, but not necessarily a realistic one.

'A shrimp of a boy, about six years old' with half of his face 'blotted out by a mulberry-coloured birthmark' has something to say (33-34). Through Piggy, the boy is able to ask what the group intend to do 'about the snake-thing' or 'beastie' (34).

Ralph insists there is no such thing, but Jack steals his thunder, saying: 'If there was a snake we'd hunt it and kill it' (35). Ralph feels 'annoyed' and momentarily 'defeated' (35). This proves there is still a power struggle going on, despite Ralph being voted the leader.

Once Ralph begins playing to his audience, he begins to win back the crowd. He tells them: 'We want to have fun. And we want to be rescued' (36). Like a populist politician, Ralph is telling the other children want they want to hear.

In order to be rescued, Ralph goes on to say that they 'must make smoke on top of the mountain' by building 'a fire' (37). Jack races off saying: 'Follow me!' (37). All the other children race off in pursuit, manically following Ralph's advice but with Jack as their leader.

Even Ralph follows the others, with Piggy bringing up the rear 'with the martyred expression of a parent who has to keep up with the senseless ebullience of the children' (38). As he is full of his auntie's wisdom, Piggy is more like an adult than any of the other children.

Ralph and Jack grin at each other, sharing 'that strange invisible light of friendship' as they work together (39). This shows how effective teamwork is, and gives hope to the pair, who have overcome their differences to unite for the common cause of building a fire.

Once Piggy arrives, Jack snatches his 'specs' to 'use them as burning glasses', as they need to ignite a flame (40). Jack is successful in producing 'a tiny flame' (40).

The danger inherent in unchecked flames is shown in this description: 'The fire thrust out a savage arm of heat that crinkled hair on the instant' (41). Not only that, the flames have been ineffective when it comes to producing smoke.

To make the fire full of smoke, Maurice suggests putting 'on green branches' (42). In the heated discussion that follows as Piggy tries to speak, Jack asserts that 'the conch doesn't count on top of the mountain' (42). Ralph disagrees and 'they assented' (42). This shows that Ralph has regained control again.

However, Jack is taking on more and more responsibility. He says his 'hunters' will 'be responsible for keeping the fire going' and 'for keeping a lookout too' (42-43). By taking on important jobs, Jack is ensuring that his power base remains intact at the very least.

Meanwhile, Roger reveals his gloomy nature by saying: 'Perhaps we'll never be rescued' (43). That gloom increases as Piggy ironically laughs, repeating: 'You got your small fire all right' (44). What follows is a forest fire, putting them all in danger.

Piggy tells them that they 'ought to be more careful' (45). He also suggests that they 'ought to have made [...] shelters' to stay warmer during the cold island nights (45). Finally, he asks where the small child 'with the mark on his face' is (46). It seems that he may have perished in the fire.

In the panic and fire that ensues, the chapter ends with 'tall swathes of creepers' rising into view, prompting the younger children to shout: 'Look at the snakes!' (47). It seems as if their worst nightmares are coming true.

Chapter Three

Jack's physical prowess is revealed from the start of this chapter, entitled: 'Huts on the Beach' (48). His stance is compared to 'a sprinter' and, later he is described as 'dog-like' (48). This makes him seem like a natural predator, as he stalks the pigs with 'a sharpened stick' (48).

This description becomes even more disturbing as we discover that his eyes are 'nearly mad' (49). Jack is relying on his instincts, shown by the description of him being 'ape-like' (49). Something sinister is implied about his behaviour, as he is described passing 'like a shadow under the darkness of the tree' (49).

Jack is all about basic survival instinct, whereas Ralph is portrayed pursuing a more peaceful activity: constructing 'a rude shelter' (50). Ralph's frustration is evident as he complains about the rest of the children 'running off' and not helping (51). Only Simon has helped.

Ignoring what Ralph is saying, while insisting that 'we want meat', shows Jack to be single-minded (51). There are also question marks about Jack's sanity, as 'the madness' comes 'into his eyes again' (51).

A conflict between the two is inevitable, as Ralph reminds Jack that he hasn't caught anything yet and they 'need shelters' (52). This causes Jack to shout 'in rage' (52).

Avoiding direct confrontation, Ralph rolls 'on his stomach' and begins playing 'with the grass' (52). This is a successful ploy, as Jack puts down his spear and begins to listen.

Simon mentions that 'the littluns' believe that 'the beastie or the snake-thing' is 'real' to back up Ralph, who is explaining to Jack that they're 'frightened' (53, 52). The omniscient narrator tells us that 'snakes were not mentioned now, we're not mentionable' (53). Snakes have become a taboo subject, it seems. The narrative draws the reader's attention to it, with repetition of two different grammatical forms of the word 'mention'.

In a strangely intimate moment, Jack admits he has fears of his own when he says that sometimes 'you can feel as if you're not hunting, but - being hunted' (53). If even the most fearless child is suffering from irrational fears, then no leap of imagination is needed to grasp how desperately the other children need a sense of safety and security. He admits: 'I know how they [the littluns] feel' (54). His empathy with them could make him more able to relate to them than Ralph, who stands more aloof with a superior sense of maturity.

Jack returns to his obsession, by saying: 'I'd like to catch a pig' (54). He prioritises that above being rescued, which infuriates Ralph, who replies: 'So long as your hunters remember the fire' (54).

The difference in their priorities leads to them talking at cross-purposes, with Ralph thinking that Jack is 'pointing' to 'a ship' rather than the pigs 'resting during the heat, like cows at home' (55). Their dispute comes to an end for now with them looking 'at each other, baffled, in love and hate' (56).

Simon, meanwhile, has drifted off 'into the forest with a sense of purpose' (57). We discover that he is 'small, skinny' with a 'pointed' chin and 'eyes so bright they had deceived Ralph into thinking him delightfully gay and wicked' (57). Below his 'coarse mop of black hair' is a 'low, broad forehead' (57). This shows there is more to Simon than initially meets the eye.

Simon's secretive nature is revealed by him secreting himself 'in a little cabin' of sorts, in the middle of 'the creepers and the bushes' (58). He is very much an individual, who does not have to seek comfort in the presence of others.

The chapter ends with images of darkness pouring out, 'submerging the ways between the trees'. Through the use of personification, the writer makes the darkness appear to be drowning the children in a sea of fear.

Chapter Four

Although the word 'whelming' is archaic, it is significant in reminding the reader that the boys are becoming engulfed by their surroundings, in this chapter entitled: 'Painted Faces and Long Hair' (60). The setting had taken over and the boys are resembling their old civilized selves less and less.

The boys are the victims of mirages, seeing what is not there, especially at 'midday' (60). They are 'menaced by the coming of the dark' (61). This shows how they are victims of their environment, particularly the littluns who are stalked by 'stomach ache and a sort of chronic diarrhoea' (61).

Roger and Maurice appear 'out of the forest' and proceed to kick down the littluns' sand castles (62). Their penchant for destruction portrays them in a negative light, especially in the case of Roger who leads 'the way' (62). Maurice has more of a conscience, as he feels 'the unease of wrong-doing' (63). In comparison, Roger seems to be the source of evil, with his 'gloomy' face and 'unsociable remoteness' that becomes something 'forbidding' (63).

Meanwhile, one of the bigger littluns, called Henry, is preoccupying himself with 'tiny transparencies' in the sea (63). He is 'a distant relative of that other boy' with the mulberry marked face', who has not been seen since the forest fire (62). This links Henry to death, and the reader may believe that his end is in sight too, especially when Roger begins stalking him.

While Henry enjoys the 'illusion of mastery', Roger begins throwing rocks towards him (64). However, Roger's arm is still 'conditioned by a civilization that knew nothing of him and was in ruins' (65). From this, we get the idea that if the boys ever return to their homes, they will find them radically changed. Despite the inherent evil that seems to exist within Roger, he is held back from committing murder by what he learned earlier in his childhood.

Jack's 'eager, impatient, beckoning' arrival redirects Roger to 'a pool at the end of the river' where Bill, Sam and Eric await (65). Jack is experimenting with clay to camouflage his appearance. Jack's subsequent 'mask' turns his laughter to 'a bloodthirsty snarling' (66). It also liberates him 'from shame and self-consciousness' (66). The reader gets the idea that Jack will not be held back by civilised notions while his face is painted; he will be more susceptible to dangerous animal instincts. What's more, the other children are powerless against it too, as 'the mask compelled them' to do its bidding (67).

Meanwhile, Piggy is thinking about making 'a sundial' (67). This makes the reader think that he is counting the hours until his return to a normal life. He has not adjusted well to this environment, which is why Ralph considers him 'a bore' (68). Of course, this is a homophone of 'boar', which implies that Piggy is a form of prey like the pigs that he shares a name with. Piggy has already been preyed upon by Jack especially, who has teased him about his weight.

By contrast, Ralph fits in perfectly; after swimming, he lays down 'sleek and streaming like a seal' (68). He is at one with the environment.

Nevertheless, Ralph wants to be rescued. When he runs 'his eye along the taut blue line of the horizon', he sees a ship in the distance (69). Consequently, Ralph runs to the top of the mountain to check whether the fire they are using as a beacon is still alight. He is oblivious to 'Henry and Johnny [...] throwing sand at Percival, but once at the top realises that the fire is 'dead' (70, 71). The personification of the fire makes the neglect of it seem all the more awful.

Ralph is so angry that he looks 'down the unfriendly side of the mountain' and clenches 'his fists' (72). He repeatedly tells Jack: 'You let the fire out', when the latter returns victoriously from his hunting expedition (73). A power struggle seems inevitable as the two boys have opposing ambitions: Jack's is to hunt, while Ralph wants to be rescued.

The complaining continues, as Ralph repeatedly tells Jack 'there was a ship' (74). Eventually, 'the dismal truth' filters 'through to everybody' (75).

However, Jack maintains that he 'needed everyone' to successfully hunt the pig (75). Rather than take on Ralph, angry Jack hits Piggy before apologising 'about the fire' (76). Significantly, Jack is not ready to apologise for his act of violence. His eyes appear 'opaque' briefly, showing that his actions are hard to understand; Ralph gently scolds Jack, saying: 'That was a dirty trick' (77).

Once the meat is being cooked, all the children partake, although Piggy has to ask: 'Aren't I having none?' (78). Kind Simon shoves 'his piece of meat over the rocks to Piggy', risking Jack's wrath (78). Indeed, the latter flings 'a great hunk of meat' at 'Simon's feet' thereafter (78).

Maurice turns peacemaker, changing the subject to 'one that could bring the majority of them together': the pig that they are eating (79). However, the subject only brings the baser elements of the children to the surface, as they chant: 'Kill the pig. Cut her throat. Bash her in' (79).

Ralph feels 'envious and resentful' and decides to call 'a meeting', leaving the chapter on a cliffhanger (79, 80). The reader can guess that Ralph will complain about the lack of civility, but we wonder how that will be received by the other children.

Chapter Five

'The tide', which is 'coming in' at the start of chapter entitled: 'Beast from Water' shows how the boys are beginning to be completely overwhelmed by their surroundings (81). Ralph chooses a 'firm strip as a path' to think (81). He needs to be on solid ground literally and metaphorically to plot the way forward, with the 'path' representing the metaphorical road ahead.

We are told that Ralph has 'discovered dirt and decay', which clearly shows he has fallen out of love with this island, that once seemed more like a paradise than hell. His views do not represent the others though, as 'to the boys' he appears as 'a darkish figure against the shimmer of the lagoon' (82). In other words, like an adult, he threatens to spoil all their fun.

Even the sunshine seems to be ready to tell the truth at this late hour, as 'now the sun was slanting in at one side [...] the shadows were where they ought to be' (83). Normally at assemblies, Ralph beholds a topsy-turvy world where the children's 'faces were lit upside down' (83). Likewise, Ralph was fond of standing on his head, earlier in the novel, indicating that he was happy in the world without parental control.

As well as noticing that this utopia is more like a dystopia, Ralph realises that he 'can't think. Not like Piggy' (83). He acknowledges Piggy's strength: 'brains' (83). This is another example of Ralph's growing maturity.

When the meeting begins, Piggy initially stands 'outside the triangle' to indicate 'that he wished to listen, but would not speak' (84). The narrator tells us that 'Piggy intended it as a gesture of disapproval' (84). Unfortunately, his protest is 'ineffectual' (85). For all his intelligence, Piggy has not been able to win the hearts and minds of the majority of the other children.

Ralph used repetition to reinforce the rules, particularly to the littluns. He has to remind them that if they're 'taken short' they should 'keep away from the fruit' (86).

He then tells the meeting that 'the fire is the most important thing on the island' (86). This comment causes 'a self-conscious giggling among the hunters', who clearly disagree with him (86).

The 'row' erupts when Ralph tells the assembled audience that they 'won't make a fire anywhere but on the mountain. Ever.' (87). That comment clearly goes against the hunters, who believe they should be able to roast whatever they catch over an open fire, wherever they happen to be.

When the topic of discussion is 'the fear', Jack stands up and takes the conch. Speaking divisively and with an accusing tone, he says: 'You littluns started all this fear talk' (88). He adds: 'Anyway, you don't hunt or build or help - you're a lot of crying babies and sissies' (88). Although, Ralph disapprovingly looks at Jack 'open-mouthed', Jack takes no notice (88). Jack clearly feels he is in control now. Jack assures them that there is 'no beast in the forest' (89).

Using a grammatically incorrect double negative, Piggy takes the conch to say 'there isn't no fear' (90). Then he adds: 'Unless we get frightened of people' (90). This is perceptive, as Jack and his hunters are what most threatens the boys' existence on the island.

Despite the older boys reading from the same hymn sheet, so to speak, a 'self-confident' littlun called 'Phil' claims he 'saw something big and horrid moving in the trees' at night (91). Simon admits it was him, adding that: 'I wanted - to go to a place - a place I know' (92).

Another littlun wants to speak up, but is intimidated by 'the assembly' chanting: 'What's your name? What's your name?' (93). He replies that it's 'Percival Wemys Madison' and begins reciting his whole address plus his telephone number (93). This reminds him he has lost his home, so he begins crying. The other littluns 'cry in sympathy' (93). Interestingly, Sir Percival in Arthurian legend is often presented as foolish but pure, a bit like the Percival in this novel.

To lighten the mood, Maurice tries to cheer them up and, although 'he clowned badly', he manages to make them laugh (94). The scene becomes more chaotic as 'without the conch', Jack begins speaking 'against the rules' (95). Jack forces Percival to say where the beast is from before reporting it to the assembly: 'He says the beast comes out of the sea' (94).

Maurice speaks with the conch in hand to say: 'My daddy says there's things, what d'you call 'em that make ink - squids - that are hundreds of yards long and eat whales whole' (95). This sets off a debate about whether or not one could come out of the sea. Although Maurice is well-intentioned and wants to help, his comment has increased the panic.

Shy Simon, meanwhile, feels 'a perilous necessity to speak' (95). He overcomes his fear of public speaking to say: 'Maybe there is a beast' (95). In the face of so much opposition, Simon becomes 'inarticulate in his effort to express mankind's essential illness' (96). He tries to ask: 'What's he dirtiest thing there is?' but the whole assembly dissolve into laughter as Jack drops 'one crude expressive syllable' (96).

Through sound imagery, the writer reminds us how threatening the island appears. 'Two grey trunks' make 'an evil squeaking that no one had noticed by day' (97). It is yet another terror of the night for the children and leads an anonymous voice to say: 'Perhaps that's what the beast is - a ghost' (97). Ralph asks for a show of hands for those who believe in ghosts. He is disappointed when he makes out the hands in the air, so he says 'flatly': 'I see' (98).

Piggy decides enough is enough and asks the assembly: 'What are we?' (98). He condemns the hunters for 'going off - hunting pigs - letting fires out', which produces an angry backlash. 'A shadow' confronts Piggy, calling him a 'fat slug' (98).

Even without the conch, Jack speaks, which makes Ralph leap to his feet to remind him of 'the rules' (99). Jack is far from listening and asserts himself, by saying: 'We're strong - we hunt' (99). By now, Jack is reduced to speaking in monosyllables, which shows how savage he has become.

The assembly scatters and Ralph has a dilemma: should he blow the conch or not? He reasons if he blows the conch and 'they don't come back', then they've 'had it' (99). In other words, they are doomed. However, Piggy's view is: 'If you don't blow, we'll soon be animals anyway' (99).

The sound of 'howling' littluns suggests that everything is now out of control. Only Simon, Ralph and Piggy remain as ineffective as 'three blind mice' (100).

Simon wisely tells Ralph to 'go on being chief', whereas Piggy worries that he'll be 'hurt' by Jack, if Ralph steps aside (101). The trio reminisce about 'home', where 'there was always a grown up' with 'an answer' (101). These comforting thoughts starkly contrast with the 'thin wail' they hear coming 'out of the darkness' (102). It turns out that it is Percival.

Chapter Six

The island inhabited by the boys has its first contact with the world outside since their arrival, in the chapter entitled: 'Beast from Air' (103). The title itself sounds superstitious, which is apt given the mental frenzy that most of the boys have whipped themselves into.

The book was published in 1954, so clearly the writer had the Cold War on his mind; the Korean War of 1950-1953 had seen Soviet Union, Chinese and North Korean troops pitted against the Americans, the British and so on, as Communist forces took on the anti-Communists. Although nuclear weapons were not used in this war, the United States had dropped two atom bombs on Japan, causing enormous devastation, to end World War Two in 1945. These events caused many to predict a bleak future with only a post-nuclear wasteland remaining after the conclusion of another full-scale war. Clearly, the writer is alluding to some kind of apocalyptic war going on, when we read of 'a sudden bright explosion and a corkscrew trail across the sky' (103). 'A figure dropping swiftly beneath a parachute' arrives on the island, which is 'a sign [...] from the world of grown ups' (103). Obviously, adults are struggling to get on with each other just as much as the boys on the island.

Meanwhile, as the dead parachutist drops, the twins, who are supposed to be looking after the fire, have 'both gone to sleep' (104). They realise that Ralph may be 'waxy' or angry at them neglecting their duty, but they snigger nonetheless (105).

As Eric watches the 'scurrying wood-lice', we can see how insignificant the boys must look from above (106). Like the wood-lice, they are trying to avoid the flames, albeit metaphorical ones of discontent now.

Once the twins hear 'the plopping noise of fabric blown open' just fifteen yards away from them, their imaginations are running wild (106). The twins wake Ralph and Piggy with news of 'the beast' and subsequently the 'darkness' is described as 'full of claws' (107).

The setting has become even more threatening because of the children's perception of it and vivid imaginations. At the hastily assembled meeting, Sam tells the others that the beast is 'furry' and has 'wings' (108). Fear has made accuracy an impossibility. Eric's face has been torn by the bushes and is 'striped with scars' (108). However, it is clear that the boys think the beast may have done it. Interestingly, the stripes make Eric seem more like a camouflaged wild animal.

Meanwhile, Jack is becoming wilder. He says: 'Sucks to the littluns', abdicating any sense of responsibility for them (110). This shows his descent into barbarism. Additionally, he shows no regard to their almost democratic process, when he says: 'We don't need the conch any more' (110-111). He seems to feel that he is more likely to get the upper hand in a state of chaos. Ralph manages to get the other boys back into line with the words: 'Don't you want to be rescued?' (111). It's a rhetorical question as no one in their right mind would answer 'no', at this stage. He then redirects Jack to the matter in hand, asking if there's 'anywhere on the island' where he hasn't been (111). This again shows how well Ralph can manage the others. Ralph allows Jack to 'lead the way' to where he thinks the beast might be, which gives the latter a sense of pride again (112).

Simon, meanwhile, suppresses 'a flicker of incredulity' (112). He cannot believe in 'a beast with claws that scratched, that sat on a mountain top, that left no tracks and yet was not fast enough to catch Samneric' (112). The twins are, of course, treated as one person now, which adds to the idea that most of the children are merging into one uncivilised mass.

Simon is unlike the others in that he thinks independent thoughts of his own. When he collides with a tree, and a 'white spot on his head' turns 'red', it seems to foreshadow his impending doom (113). He is literally and metaphorically out of step with the others, so a fatal collision is likely.

As the boys near the site where the beast might be, Ralph takes control. He listens to the voice 'deep' inside him, which says to the others: 'I'm chief. I'll go. Don't argue' (114). Using short sentences, Ralph appears commanding and in control to the other boys. However, Jack follows him, telling him: 'Couldn't let you do it on your own' (115). Rather than fearing for Ralph's safety, Jack fears for his own leadership so feels compelled to join Ralph or risk undermining his own position as a fearless leader.

The old conflict between them rises to the surface as Ralph observes that 'there's no signal now' (116). Jack still fails to see the importance of maintaining the fire and smoke to ensure they have a better chance of being rescued. This is exemplified when he replies: 'You're nuts on the signal' (116). Instead, much to Ralph's disgust, Jack and his followers 'go wasting' their time, rolling rocks (117).

Chaos ensues as Roger claims they have 'plenty of time' and all the boys go in different directions: some 'to the beach', while some want 'to roll more rocks' (118). The latter group seem to be on an inexorable path to wanton self-destruction.

To end the chapter, there's a play on words, as Ralph asks: 'Are you all off your rockers?' (118). This rhetorical question is ineffective at bringing them back into the fold, as 'mutinously, the boys' fall 'silent or muttering' (118). This indicates that Ralph is losing his power over them.

Chapter Seven

This chapter, entitled 'Shadows and Tall Trees', starts with Ralph following Jack along 'the pig-run' (119). However, Ralph is not a follower, retaining a much stronger link with the civilised behaviour the boys have left behind. This is notable when he plans 'his toilet' (119). He longs for 'a pair of scissors' to cut his hair (119).

After realising he has bitten his nails 'to the quick', he becomes self-deprecating, musing to himself: 'Be sucking my thumb next -' (119, 120). Ralph realises that he is going backward through evolution by being in this environment. Not surprisingly, this brings on a wave of pessimism as he stares out at the 'brute obtuseness of the ocean' and feels 'helpless' and 'condemned' (121).

However, Ralph is a born survivor and is ready to adapt to stay alive on the island. He embraces the spirit of compromise as he agrees with Jack that if he means 'going the right way, [to the beast] we'll hunt' (122). Although he drifts off into reminiscing about books of his childhood, he still manages to hurl a 'foolish wooden stick' at a boar (123). This description suggests his heart is not completely in hunting. Nevertheless, he does have mixed feelings as he is described as 'full of fright and apprehension and pride' (124). The repetition of 'and' shows how these emotions are accumulating to make him confused. He even gets 'carried away by a sudden thick excitement' and jabs at Robert with Eric's spear (125). Robert cries after getting hurt, but Ralph sees it as 'just a game' (126). However, he says this 'uneasily' suggesting that he feels guilty (126).

Meanwhile, Jack is much more brutal. He believes that he and his hunters can 'kill' the beast (127). He is much more sure of himself than Ralph. He is not riddled with self-doubt like Ralph, who thinks 'he would never be a good chess player' (128). Despite his shortcomings, Ralph is driven by his sense of responsibility, which is lacking in Jack.

Ralph tries hard to manage Jack, sensing his 'rising antagonism, understanding that this was how Jack felt as soon as he ceased to lead' (129). However, the tension rises as Jack insinuates that Ralph is 'frightened' of climbing the mountain that evening (130). He stays 'cool and casual' so Jack's taunting falls 'powerless' (131).

Eventually, Jack goes up alone and is described as a 'stain', detaching itself and drawing away. He returns shortly afterwards saying he 'saw a thing bulge on the mountain' (133). Ralph becomes almost parental thereafter, taking the upper hand, telling Jack and Roger: 'We'll go and look' (133). When he sees the sight that Jack saw, Ralph's courage deserts him and he has to smother 'a cry' (134). He has to appear tough to the others, so cannot openly show cowardice.

Nevertheless, the sight of 'something like a great ape' is disturbing for all three of them (135). After the encounter, all that is left are 'three abandoned sticks and the thing that bowed' (135). The word 'bowed' shows that this thing is about to take on religious significance for the boys.

Chapter Eight

Chapter eight, entitled 'Gift for the Darkness' begins with Piggy looking 'up miserably from the dawn-pale beach to the dark mountain' (136). This may suggest that the civilised values he represents are running out of energy, while only a 'dark' future looms over him. Using the setting, the writer foreshadows Piggy's doom.

Ralph realises that light is important, both metaphorically and literally. This is shown when he talks about their fear of the beast, saying: 'As long as there's light we're brave enough' (137). Meanwhile, Jack remains fixated on his 'hunters', who are dismissed as 'boys armed with sticks' by Ralph (137). This causes a huge rift between the two of them.

It turns into a propaganda war, as Jack uses the symbol of democracy, the conch, to manipulate his audience. Although he is lying, he claims that Ralph said his 'hunters are no good' and called them 'cowards' (138).

Jack tries to undermine Ralph's authority, by saying: 'He isn't a proper chief' (138).

Initially, the boys stay loyal to Ralph, which causes Jack to speak 'in tones of deep meaning, and menace' (139). He even stabs 'the air with his index finger' as he talks (139). His level of aggression is obvious.

However, he suffers a humiliating defeat, which causes him to blunder 'out of the triangle towards the drop to the white sand'. It is clear that Jack is sinking morally literally and metaphorically (140).

With Jack gone, Simon tries to speak up, but is met with 'a half-sound of jeering' (141). The worse aspects of a crowd mentality are already revealing themselves to the reader, who is likely to feel sympathy for Simon, who 'shrank' from the sound (141).

Piggy demonstrates his higher-level thinking skills when he suggests moving the fire to the beach, on account of the beast. The reader discovers that in Jack's absence, Piggy's 'liberty' is 'expanding' (142).

The remaining boys are still trying to cling onto the vestiges of civilization. That is shown when they build 'a pyramid of leaves and twigs' (143). Piggy has moved to centre stage 'for the first time on the island', as he manipulates his 'one glass' to produce fire.
Ralph is clearly feeling the stress of his position, as there is 'a drop of blood' on the sand, due to him biting his

nails (144). The writer is foreshadowing the bloodshed on the horizon.

Not only is he stressed, but Ralph appears to be losing his sanity as it takes him time to remember 'what had been worrying him': it is Simon's disappearance (145). Ironically, Piggy says Simon is 'cracked', when it is Ralph who is cracking up mentally (145).

Simon, meanwhile, has 'crawled' inside 'the great mat', which is his secret hiding place (146). Although he seems to feel secure there, 'the arrow of the sun' which falls upon indicates otherwise (146).

Ideas around death are evoked again, as each of Jack's 'hunters' are pictured wearing 'the remains of a black cap' (146). It signifies death, as judges used to don a black cap before announcing that capital punishment would be the punishment for a defendant.

Like Simon in the earlier scene, the pigs that Jack's followers are hunting are 'enjoying the shadows under the trees' (147). It seems that a similar fate will await Simon.

Jack's descent into savagery is exemplified by his primitive beliefs. He believes that by making a sacrifice to the beast then it 'won't bother' them (147). He adds the word 'maybe', showing that he's afraid himself of the beast and wants to placate it.

The savagery of the hunters is emphasised when we begin to see the sow's plight partly from her perspective. The omniscient narrator explains that the spears embedded in her flesh are a 'torment' (148). This makes the reader feel sympathy for the poor injured animal. Not only that, but the hunters are portrayed negatively as 'wedded to her in lust' (148). This suggests that they are just as animalistic.

Again, the reader is subtly reminded of Simon, as 'the butterflies still danced' as the sow dies (149). This beautiful imagery is juxtaposed with the boys' callousness as Robert's crude phrase: 'Right up her ass' is 'received uproariously' (149).

Meanwhile, the beast is becoming more and more revered. This is exemplified when Jack speaks in 'lower' tones, when referring to it (150). It is now a taboo word as Jack says: 'We'll leave part of the kill for - ' (150).

The head of the sow, which suggests the boys are sacrificing their brains to their primitive God, is planted in the ground on a stick. There is nothing beautiful about this sacrifice, which Simon can see from his lair. It is so awful that: 'Even the butterflies' desert the 'open space where the obscene thing' grins (151).

Simon is very much affected by this gory vision, which is named 'the Lord of the Flies' by the omniscient narrator (152). The tribal and religious nature of the sacrifice is emphasised by how 'a pulse' begins 'to beat' in Simon's 'right temple' (152). This implies that even he is being brought down by the imaginary tribal drums that seem to beat in this place.

Meanwhile, Ralph is perturbed when he realises 'how little he thought like a grown-up' (153). However, at least he is trying to be responsible, hoping he can rise above the animal natures of those around him.

While the beast is taboo for the hunters, for Ralph and Piggy it's Jack. The narrator reveals: 'A taboo was evolving round that word too' (154). This shows how big a threat Jack is to their continued existence as civilised beings on this island.

'Thunder' booms as Jack and his hunters raid Ralph's camp (155). The weather conditions are often considered as an example of pathetic fallacy, indicating that the main protagonist is in serious danger.

The pressure seems to be closing Ralph down mentally. The narrator reveals that 'the shutter [in his brain] had come down' (156). He seems mentally feeble now, as he needs Piggy to prompt him when he forgets why they need to 'keep the fire burning' (156).

Meanwhile, Simon is engaging in an imaginary conversation with the Lord of the Flies. His lack of confidence is clear, as it calls him 'batty' (157). Simon is hallucinating as he sees the Lord of the Flies 'expanding like a balloon' (158). It is no surprise when he literally loses 'consciousness' (159). Metaphorically, it reminds us that the hunters have already lost their ability to make conscious decisions, they are simply operating on instinct alone.

Chapter Nine

The tension increases in chapter nine, entitled: 'A View to a Death', as we are told 'the air was ready to explode' (160). Through pathetic fallacy, the writer is preparing the reader for the violence to come. Additionally, 'blood' gushes out of Simon's nose, foreshadowing his fate (160).

Simon appears to be reaching the end of his life, as he displays 'a sort of glum determination like an old man' (161). Shortly afterwards, his frailty and similarity to an animal is emphasised by him kneeling 'on all fours' to vomit (162). Clearly, this is more evidence of foreshadowing.

The oppressive air is even affecting Piggy, who says: 'I wish the air was cooler' (163). Together with Ralph, he is becoming more like the hunters in this environment, which is evident when they 'both giggled like Sam' (164).

Jack, meanwhile, is portrayed as 'painted and garlanded', sitting 'there like an idol' (164). He is lord over all he surveys. He graciously allows Ralph and Piggy to have some meat. The narrative emphasises Jack's position by personifying it thus: 'Power lay in the brown swell of his forearms' (165). We get the feeling that Jack has become more physically powerful, possibly a by-product of hunting.

This is a world where normal rules do not apply, as Jack reminds Ralph: 'The conch doesn't count at this end of the island' (166). However, Ralph disputes this which increases the tension.

As the rain falls, Jack's shortcomings as leader come to the fore, as he has not made any preparations for poor weather conditions. Ralph pushes home his advantage by saying: 'Who's clever now? Where are your shelters?' (167).

Without shelters to run to, all vestiges of civilisation are lost and the children engage in a ritualised 'dance' (167). Even 'Piggy and Ralph, under the threat of the sky', find 'themselves eager to take a place in this demented but partly secure society' (167). It seems that they are enjoying a feeling of safety in numbers.

The subsequent chanting is reminiscent of the thumping in Simon's head earlier in the narrative, as we are told it 'began to beat like a steady pulse' (168). The circle of boys becomes 'a horseshoe' shape, which usually represents luck. Ironically, it is a foreboding shape for Simon, described as 'a thing', who stumbles in (168).

The boys savage Simon 'tearing' him apart with 'teeth and claws' (169). Once Simon is dead, the boys realise 'how small a beast it was' (169). Meanwhile, the former beast, the dead parachutist is blown 'out to sea' (169).

Now dead, Simon appears to be turning into a monument, symbolising the error of the boys' ways. His shoulder becomes 'sculptured marble' and 'his cheek silvered' (170). The only winner is the environment, as Simon's body moves out 'towards the open sea', surrounded 'by a fringe of inquisitive bright creatures' (170).

Chapter Ten

Chapter ten, entitled 'The Shell and the Glasses', begins by showing a Piggy's-eye-view of Ralph. The main protagonist cuts a sorry figure, 'limping, dirty, with dead leaves hanging from his shock of yellow hair' (171). We feel sympathy for this victim of an extremely harsh environment.

Ralph's been mentally affected too. We notice how cynical he has become when he laughs 'sharply' at Piggy's suggestion that they could 'call an assembly' (172). Ralph realises he has lost control of the other boys, apart from Piggy, and to a lesser extent, Sam and Eric.

Piggy seems the more powerful character, at this point in the novel. We see Piggy standing 'over Ralph' (173). He's more lucid than Ralph who, unlike Piggy, won't admit he was 'scared' when Simon was killed during 'that bloody dance' (173).

Ralph's declining power is emphasised when Sam and Eric look 'past him into the air' when they encounter him (174).

The threat of future violence lingers as the narrator reports that 'the air was heavy with unspoken knowledge' (175). These taboo subjects add gothic tension to the plot.

Ralph's powerlessness is juxtaposed with Jack's increasing ability to wield power. Roger admits how much he admires Jack when says to Robert: 'He's a proper Chief, isn't he?' (176). However, Jack is a brutal chief, as even Roger assimilates 'the possibilities of irresponsible authority', with Wilfred waiting for a beating (176).

Despite this view, Jack has learned from his mistake of not constructing a shelter. He orders some of his followers to 'improve the cave' while he and his hunters look for pigs (177). Bill points out that a feast will be impossible if they can't cook the meat. The mask of 'white and red clay' covers his embarrassment as Jack realises he needs to raid the other camp to get fire (178).

Meanwhile, Ralph and Piggy discuss 'the double function of the fire' (179). They realise they need it as a 'hearth' to comfort them in this inhospitable environment as well as signalling to the outside world that they want to be rescued (179).

Sam and Eric have to be convincing of the need to maintain the fire. Piggy takes up the role of a responsible teacher, saying: 'How else are we going to be rescued?' The rhetorical question forces them to agree that the fire is the only option if they want to escape.

Soon they give into the darkness and all it represents, as even Piggy admits: 'Nobody ain't going to see smoke in the dark' (181). Slowly, even these boys are giving up their hold on civilisation.

Ralph's only connection with civilisation is through 'his nightly game of supposing' (182). In his imagination, Ralph is in Devon.

Ralph's reverie is interrupted by Sam and Eric 'fighting each other' (182). This foreshadows what is about to happen.

Escapism through humour is Ralph's next attempt to forget his immediate environment. A 'tiny joke' makes him snigger uncontrollably (183). He is clearly losing his grip on reality.

While they are trying to sleep, 'Ralph and Piggy's corner' becomes 'a complication of snarls and crashes and flying limbs' (184). The accumulation of violence is emphasised by the repetition of the word 'and' (184). The simile of the fist withdrawing and coming 'back like a piston' reminds us of how unthinking the boys are now.

The chapter ends with Jack, who is now referred to as 'The Chief' dangling 'Piggy's broken glasses' from his left hand (186). He exults 'in his achievement', knowing that he has all the power in his hands now (186).

Chapter Eleven

This chapter, entitled 'Castle Rock', establishes the theme of death from the onset with Ralph blowing the 'grey, feathery ashes' of the fire that has gone out (187). All hope is deserting them now that they are without the means of creating a new fire.

Ralph is abdicating responsibility at this point in the narrative as he pushes 'the conch into Piggy's hands' to call an assembly (188). Piggy empowers Ralph again by 'snivelling', allowing him to take command again (188).

However, to Piggy it's 'jus' talk without deciding' (189). Sam suggests that they 'take spears' if they are going to Jack's camp to recover Piggy's glasses (189). Sam wants to fight violence with violence and is more decisive than

Ralph, who wants to go there with 'hair brushed' (189). Ralph has become a passive and impractical victim.

Sam is afraid of Jack, as he'll be 'painted' and might get 'waxy' (190). All of them understand 'the liberation into savagery' brought about by 'the concealing paint' (191). Ralph refuses to ape Jack's gang by wearing paint too, saying: 'We aren't savages' (191).

Ralph is struggling to remember why they have to maintain the fire, by Piggy gently reminds him. To boost Ralph's flagging confidence, Piggy says: 'You remember everything' (192).

Jack's camp in Castle Rock is a gothic setting, with its 'mass of twisted stems' (193). It seems to be an evil place. Something terrible is taking over the boys there, especially Roger, who feels a 'source of power' pulsing in his body (194).

The conflict between Jack and Ralph escalates as the latter's temper blazes, when he demands the return of 'Piggy's specs' (195). A fight between the two ensues, but they still retain some connection with civilization as evidence by the fact that 'by common consent' they use 'spears as sabres' (196). Clearly, they don't want to mortally wound each other.

Ralph's mental state is still weakened after the fight as we discover that his mind 'faltered' when he tries to speak (197). He still needs Piggy's prompts.

His position is weakened further as Samneric are captured. The hunters feel the twins' 'otherness' (198). Clearly, they want everyone to conform with their way of living.

Nevertheless, Ralph's 'temper' breaks again (199). He charges at Jack, who charges back. All the while, Roger, who is stationed above, is tossing stones at those below.

Piggy makes arguably his most effective speech, with three rhetorical questions all beginning with the words: 'Which is better' (200). Roger puts an end to it, by releasing a huge stone, which crushes Piggy and any hope of returning to civilized ways.

As Ralph is pursued, 'a great noise as of sea-gulls' reminds us how vicious and predatory Jack's hunters have become (201). Roger, in particular, seems devoid of any morals as he looks down on the captive twins, surveying them 'as one wielding a nameless authority' (202).

Chapter Twelve

The final chapter, entitled 'Cry of the Hunters', begins with Ralph lying 'in a covert' (203). This setting marks him out as prey, as a covert is a thicket where game can hide.

Ralph ponders his bleak future and predicts the 'painted savages' will go 'further and further' (204). By not specifying the lengths that Jack's hunters will go to the narrative depicts a terrifying and unknown end to the novel.

The idea of the outcast, similar to that found in 'Frankenstein' is explored again, as Ralph is surprised that 'two littluns' run and scream upon seeing him (205). Ralph's appearance is now almost monstrous to them.

Clearly, the boys' vivid imaginations have been whipped up into a frenzy by Jack and the harshness of the environment they are enduring. Superstition is rife and even affects Ralph when he feels he has to back away from the Lord of the Flies, 'keeping his face to the skull that lay grinning at the sky' (206).

Now that he's an outcast, he seems more like Piggy. This idea is emphasised when he edges his way forward near Castle Rock 'as though he were blind' in the darkness (207).

He tries to speak to Samneric, as they are the only potential allies that are left. Ralph is losing the power of expression, as he ends up repeating: 'I came to see you two -' (208). He is no longer articulate; he is succumbing to the lack of civilisation around him.

Ralph is being treated like a hunted animal, as Samneric tell him that they've been instructed to throw their 'spears like at a pig' (209). They warn him of Roger, particularly, who's 'a terror' (210). Ominously, they add that: 'Roger sharpened a stick at both ends' (211). We can only assume that Ralph's death will be especially grisly, if he Roger has anything to do with it. The gothic, unknown terror of the spoken heightens the tension.

Nevertheless, Ralph's survival instincts kick in, as he attempts to retain a sense of optimism. He hatches a plan of sorts, believing naively that he will be 'free' if he stays in his 'lair' (212). He feels 'secure, and clever' in the ferns (213. Defiantly, he picks up his stick, ready for 'battle' (214). As readers, we cannot judge him, as he has been pushed to these extremes; no amount of reasoning will work with Jack and his followers.

Ralph's pursuers try to kill him by launching huge rocks from above. The tension rises as the narrator reveals that Ralph's 'heart-beats were visible' (215). His animal instincts are keeping him alive as he shows 'his teeth' at a wall of branches, before snarling and waiting for his pursuers (216). When he encounters one of his pursuers, he launches 'himself like a cat' (217).

He is all too aware that his human side is in decline. Ralph fears that 'the curtain' may 'waver in his brain', reducing him to a 'simpleton' (218). However, simpletons are flourishing here, so Ralph's resorting to animalistic behaviour is his only hope of survival.

Eventually, Ralph stumbles onto what appears to be Simon's old hideout, where 'bushes and a wild tangle of creeper made a mat that kept out all the light of the sun' (219). The lack of sunlight and the 'mat', which indicates it is underfoot, makes this seem like a natural graveyard (219).

Ralph is stirred by the fire lit by his pursuers and his fear of 'a stick sharpened at both ends', which is repeated in the narrative (220). Sound imagery heightens the tension, as the reader can imagine the cacophony produced by the 'screaming' birds and the 'shrieking' mice (221). When Ralph encounters a 'savage' with a 'stake sharpened at both ends', we can completely understand why he elects to charge him (221). It is either kill or be killed.

He eventually stumbles over in the sand, as he makes his way onto the beach. When he looks up 'at a huge peaked cap', the imagery is very natural as we discover the hat's 'green shade' and 'gold foliage' (222). It is almost as if Ralph can no longer remember anything from his previous life, so this naval uniform is not instantly recognisable.

Ironically, the huge fire created by Jack and his followers to hunt Ralph has raged out of control and alerted rescuers. The officer asks 'cheerfully' if they have been 'having a war or something' (223). Clearly, the officer can have no idea how close to the truth he is.

Percival Wemy Madison attempts to speak to the officer, but fails miserably. His powers of communication let him down. Interestingly, he searches 'in his head for an incantation that had faded clean away' (224). This shows how much trust he has in magic and chanting. His connection with civilisation has completely faded away.

The novel ends with Ralph's weeping 'for the end of innocence, the darkness of man's heart, and the fall through the air of the true, wise friend called Piggy'

(225). He seems most traumatised by the latter, as that makes up the last part of this ascending tricolon.

Essay writing tips
Use a variety of connectives

Have a look of this list of connectives. Which of these would you choose to use?

'ADDING' DISCOURSE MARKERS

- AND

- ALSO

- AS WELL AS

- MOREOVER

- TOO

- FURTHERMORE

- ADDITIONALLY

I hope you chose 'additionally', 'furthermore' and 'moreover'. Don't be afraid to use the lesser discourse markers, as they are also useful. Just avoid using those ones over and over again. I've seen essays from Key Stage 4 students that use the same discourse marker for the opening sentence of each paragraph! Needless to say, those essays didn't get great marks!

Okay, here are some more connectives for you to look at. Select the best ones.

'SEQUENCING' DISCOURSE MARKERS

- NEXT

- FIRSTLY

- SECONDLY

- THIRDLY

- FINALLY

- MEANWHILE

- AFTER

- THEN

- SUBSEQUENTLY

This time, I hope you chose 'subsequently' and 'meanwhile'.

Here are some more connectives for you to 'grade'!

'ILLUSTRATING / EXEMPLIFYING' DISCOURSE MARKERS

- FOR EXAMPLE

- SUCH AS

- FOR INSTANCE

- IN THE CASE OF

- AS REVEALED BY

- ILLUSTRATED BY

I'd probably go for 'illustrated by' or even 'as exemplified by' (which is not in the list!). Please feel free to add your own examples to the lists. Strong connectives impress examiners. Don't forget it! That's why I want you to look at some more.

'CAUSE & EFFECT' DISCOURSE MARKERS

- BECAUSE

- SO

- THEREFORE

- THUS

- CONSEQUENTLY

- HENCE

I'm going for 'consequently' this time. How about you? What about the next batch?

'COMPARING' DISCOURSE MARKERS

- SIMILARLY

- LIKEWISE

- AS WITH

- LIKE

- EQUALLY

- IN THE SAME WAY

I'd choose 'similarly' this time. Still some more to go.

'QUALIFYING' DISCOURSE MARKERS

- BUT

- HOWEVER

- WHILE

- ALTHOUGH

- UNLESS

- EXCEPT

- APART FROM

- AS LONG AS

It's 'however' for me!

'CONTRASTING' DISCOURSE MARKERS

- WHEREAS

- INSTEAD OF

- ALTERNATIVELY

- OTHERWISE

- UNLIKE

- ON THE OTHER HAND

- CONVERSELY

I'll take 'conversely' or 'alternatively' this time.

'EMPHASISING' DISCOURSE MARKERS

- ABOVE ALL

- IN PARTICULAR

- ESPECIALLY

- SIGNIFICANTLY

- INDEED

- NOTABLY

You can breathe a sigh of relief now! It's over! No more connectives. However, now I want to put our new found skills to use in our essays.

Useful information/Glossary

Allegory: extended metaphor, like the grim reaper representing death, e.g. Scrooge symbolizing capitalism.

Alliteration: same consonant sound repeating, e.g. 'She sells sea shells'.

Allusion: reference to another text/person/place/event.

Ascending tricolon: sentence with three parts, each increasing in power, e.g. 'ringing, drumming, shouting'.

Aside: character speaking so some characters cannot hear what is being said. Sometimes, an aside is directly to the audience. It's a dramatic technique which reveals the character's inner thoughts and feelings.

Assonance: same vowel sounds repeating, e.g. 'Oh no, won't Joe go?'

Bathos: abrupt change from sublime to ridiculous for humorous effect.

Blank verse: lines of unrhymed iambic pentameter.

Compressed time: when the narrative is fast-forwarding through the action.

Descending tricolon: sentence with three parts, each decreasing in power, e.g. 'shouting, talking, whispering'.

Denouement: tying up loose ends, the resolution.

Diction: choice of words or vocabulary.

Didactic: used to describe literature designed to inform, instruct or pass on a moral message.

Dilated time: opposite compressed time, here the narrative is in slow motion.

Direct address: second person narrative, predominantly using the personal pronoun 'you'.

Dramatic action verb: manifests itself in physical action, e.g. I punched him in the face.

Dramatic irony: audience knows something that the character is unaware of.

Ellipsis: leaving out part of the story and allowing the reader to fill in the narrative gap.

End-stopped lines: poetic lines that end with punctuation.

Epistolary: letter or correspondence-driven narrative.

Flashback/Analepsis: going back in time to the past, interrupting the chronological sequence.

Flashforward/Prolepsis: going forward in time to the future, interrupting the chronological sequence.

Foreshadowing/Adumbrating: suggestion of plot developments that will occur later in the narrative.

Gothic: another strand of Romanticism, typically with a wild setting, a sensitive heroine, an older man with a 'piercing gaze', discontinuous structure, doppelgangers, guilt and the 'unspeakable' (according to Eve Kosofsky Sedgwick).

Hamartia: character flaw, leading to that character's downfall.

Hyperbole: exaggeration for effect.

Iambic pentameter: a line of ten syllables beginning with a lighter stress alternating with a heavier stress in its perfect form, which sounds like a heartbeat. The stress falls on the even syllables, numbers: 2, 4, 6, 8 and 10, e.g. 'When now I think you can behold such sights'.

Intertextuality: links to other literary texts.

Irony: amusing or cruel reversal of expected outcome or words meaning the opposite to their literal meaning.

Metafiction/Romantic irony: self-conscious exposure of the devices used to create 'the truth' within a work of fiction.

Motif: recurring image use of language or idea that connects the narrative together and creates a theme or mood, e.g. 'green light' in *The Great Gatsby*.

Objective correlative: external features of the scene mirroring the feelings of a character.

Oxymoron: contradictory terms combined, e.g. deafening silence.

Pastiche: imitation of another's work.

Pathetic fallacy: a form of personification whereby inanimate objects show human attributes, e.g. 'the sea smiled benignly'. The originator of the term, John Ruskin in 1856, used 'the cruel, crawling foam', from Kingsley's *The Sands of Dee*, as an example to clarify what he meant by the 'morbid' nature of pathetic fallacy.

Personification: concrete or abstract object made human, often simply achieved by using a capital letter or a personal pronoun, e.g. 'Nature', or describing a ship as 'she'.

Pun/Double entendre: a word with a double meaning, usually employed in witty wordplay but not always.

Retrospective: account of events after they have occurred.

Romanticism: genre celebrating the power of imagination, spriritualism and nature.

Semantic/lexical field: related words about a single concept, e.g. king, queen and prince are all concerned with royalty.

Soliloquy: character thinks aloud, but is not heard by other characters (unlike in a monologue) giving the audience access to inner thoughts and feelings.

Style: choice of language, form and structure, and effects produced.

Synecdoche: one part of something referring to the whole, e.g. Carker's teeth represent him in *Dombey and Son*.

Syntax: the way words and sentences are placed together.

Tetracolon climax: sentence with four parts, culminating with the last part, e.g. 'I have nothing to offer but blood, toil, tears, and sweat' (Winston Churchill).

ABOUT THE AUTHOR

Joe Broadfoot is a secondary school teacher of English and a soccer journalist, who also writes fiction and literary criticism. His former experiences as a DJ took him to far-flung places such as Tokyo, Kobe, Beijing, Hong Kong, Jakarta, Cairo, Dubai, Cannes, Oslo, Bergen and Bodo. He is now PGCE and CELTA-qualified with QTS, a first-class honours degree in Literature and an MA in Victorian Studies (majoring in Charles Dickens). Drama is close to his heart as he acted in 'Macbeth' and 'A Midsummer Night's Dream' at the Royal Northern College of Music in Manchester. More recently, he has been teaching 'A' Level and GCSE English Literature and IGCSE and GCSE English Language to students at secondary schools in Buckinghamshire, Kent and in south and west London.

19422454R00043

Printed in Poland
by Amazon Fulfillment
Poland Sp. z o.o., Wrocław